Can I Catch a Cold from the Cold?

A Children's Disease Book (Learning About Diseases)

BABY PROFESSOR

EDUCATION KIDS

Speedy Publishing LLC
40 E. Main St. #1156
Newark, DE 19711
www.speedypublishing.com

We commonly here mothers say, it's so cold outside. You should not go out and play because you might catch cold, or, stay indoors during winter so you won't get sick and catch cold.

Does cold weather really cause colds or other sickness?

Among all the much talked about beliefs about colds, this one is very persistent. Many people think that when you get exposed to the cold environment, you can catch a cold.

However, according
to the doctors,
you only get colds
when you have
been infected by
a cold virus. Cold
temperature in a
room, or the cold
weather outside,
does not cause
the sickness.

Cold air could
irritate your
nostrils and make
you sneeze. But
sneezing does
not mean that
you have a cold.

So how will I know
the symptoms
that tell me I am
catching a cold?

When you
have sneezing,
coughing, fever
and possibly
chills, then you
are infected by a
cold virus. There
is inflammation
in the mucous
membranes that
line the respiratory
passages, where
air goes when
you breathe.

But why is it that colds and flu seem to be common during cold weather?

When a person
who has a cold, or
someone who has
a respiratory virus,
sneezes, the cold virus
is pushed out into the
air as a small droplet.
It stays longer in the
air in cold weather.

When the virus
is inhaled by
another person,
it can cause that
person to get
sick with a cold.

Another reason why colds and flu are common in the winter season is that as more people restrict themselves to stay indoors, the greater the chance that a virus could be spread because of the close contact of people staying together indoors.

Does that mean
that it's okay to
play outside even
when it's cold?

Extreme temperatures outside can be dangerous for newborns, the elderly and those who may have certain medical conditions.

But kids and adults
who are healthy
and are properly
dressed and
know how to use
good judgment
can certainly
play and stay
active outdoors.

Just remember to dress for the weather. Protect your face, keep moving, warm up with hot drinks, stay closer to home and know when it's time to quit and go indoors.

In conclusion,
it's not true that
the change in the
temperature causes
people to catch
colds. You catch
a cold when you
inhale a cold virus.

So to keep
yourself away
from getting a
cold virus, keep
a safe distance
from people who
have colds.

Visit

www.BabyProfessorBooks.com

to download Free Baby Professor eBooks
and view our catalog of new and exciting
Children's Books